Governor
Ralph Carr

Defender of Japanese Americans

D1523592

Governor
Ralph Carr

Defender of Japanese Americans

by E. E. Duncan

Filter Press, LLC
Palmer Lake, Colorado

Governor Ralph Carr:
Defender of Japanese Americans
by E. E. Duncan

Published by Filter Press, LLC, in cooperation with
Denver Public Schools and Colorado Humanities

ISBN: 978-086541-116-6
LCCN: 2011924856

Produced with the support of Colorado Humanities and the
National Endowment for the Humanities. Any views, findings,
conclusions, or recommendations expressed in this publication
do not necessarily represent those of the National Endowment
for the Humanities or Colorado Humanities.

Cover photograph courtesy History Colorado, 10028117.

Printed in the United States of America

Great Lives in Colorado History Series

For information on upcoming titles,
contact *info@FilterPressBooks.com*.

Contents

*Colorado Governor Ralph Carr is remembered for defending
the rights of Japanese Americans during World War II.
Governor Carr had a boyish round face and a big smile.*

Ralph Carr

Colorado Governor Ralph Carr stood up for his beliefs. During **World War II**, the United States was at war with Japan. Most Americans saw *all* Japanese people, including **Japanese Americans**, as the enemy. Ralph Carr believed Japanese Americans should have the same rights as all other Americans. Most people in Colorado disagreed with Ralph Carr, but he stayed true to his beliefs.

On December 7, 1941, Japanese airplanes swooped down from the sky. They dropped bombs on **Pearl Harbor**, a naval base in Hawaii. More than 3,500 Navy workers were killed or hurt. Ships, airplanes, and buildings were destroyed. Now, Japan and America were at war. Later, in the same war, America would also fight against Germany and Italy.

Many Japanese people lived in California. Most were born in America and were U.S.

citizens. America was their home and their country. Because the United States was at war with Japan during World War II, people hated and feared all Japanese people. There was **prejudice** and **discrimination** against Japanese Americans because they looked like the enemy the United States was fighting in the war.

Ralph Carr believed that American citizens should not be judged by the way they looked. He knew that all American citizens had rights. Carr fought against the prejudice and discrimination the Japanese Americans experienced during World War II.

Early Years

Ralph Carr was born in the tiny mining town of Rosita, Colorado, on December 11, 1887. His father was a miner. During his childhood, his family moved to a silver camp in Aspen, then to a gold camp in Cripple Creek. His father never struck it rich, and the family was poor. The family's homes were little log cabins in the mountains. At age six, Ralph started

Courtesy DPL, Western History Collection, X-703

The Carr family cabin in Cripple Creek was located behind the cabin in this picture. Life in Cripple Creek, Colorado, in the 1890s was difficult. The Carr family struggled to make a living in the gold mining town.

Ralph Carr as a young man.

4 *Ralph Carr*

working to help his family. He carried gold samples from the mines and sold newspapers.

People from all over the world lived in the mining camps of Colorado. Ralph met people from other countries. He learned that America was a place where people from different backgrounds and countries could live and work together.

Ralph was an excellent student. He enjoyed writing, reading, and Latin. He graduated

Courtesy DPL, Western History Collection, P-792

Ralph graduated from Cripple Creek High School in 1905.

from Cripple Creek High School in 1905 and earned a scholarship to attend the University of Colorado. Ralph was a very good writer. He wrote articles for the college newspaper. He surprised everyone when he decided to go to law school instead of becoming a newspaper reporter. He received his law degree in 1912.

Life in the San Luis Valley

Ralph met and fell in love with Gretchen
Fowler while they were students at the
University of Colorado. They married and
adopted two children, Robert and Cynthia.
They moved to the town of Antonito,
Colorado. He worked as a lawyer. Ralph
taught himself Spanish to help people in the
Hispanic communities of the San Luis Valley.
He also met people in the small Japanese-
American community near Antonito.

Ralph Carr was a friendly man and popular
in his community. He wore a cowboy hat
and had a big smile. He loved the Colorado
outdoors and relaxed by fishing. He often
took his children with him when he fished.

Ralph studied the life of President Abraham
Lincoln. He admired President Lincoln
because Lincoln believed in **liberty** and

democracy. President Lincoln defended the rights of African Americans in the American Civil War. Ralph wrote articles for magazines about Lincoln.

He also was interested in what made Americans special. In a magazine article, Ralph wrote, "When we [new **immigrants**] reach the U.S., we are transformed into new people, and we have left behind us everything. We have become new men and women with new interests, **devotions**, and **loyalties**." His belief that people who come to America leave behind their old loyalties and become Americans helped him support and defend Japanese Americans during World War II.

Governor Carr

After 11 years in Antonito, Ralph moved his family to Denver. He worked as Colorado's assistant **attorney general**. He did a good job, and in 1929, President Herbert Hoover selected him to be the U.S. attorney for Colorado. Ralph Carr and President Herbert Hoover remained friends for the rest of Ralph's life. During the time Ralph was serving as U.S. attorney, his wife died of diabetes, and he became a single father of his two teenage children. Gretchen's death was sudden and unexpected, and Ralph was very sad. Eleven years later, soon after World War II ended, Ralph Carr met and married his second wife, Eleanor Fairall Carr. He called her the "loveliest little lady in Colorado."

Some friends asked him to run for governor of Colorado. He liked the idea. In 1938, Ralph Carr was elected. He was a Republican.

African American and Hispanic voters helped him win the election. Ralph was popular because he supported the rights of working people and because he was an **ethical** man. Ralph was elected for two years, then re-elected for two more years.

Japanese Americans during World War II

While Ralph was governor, Japan attacked Pearl Harbor. People thought Japanese Americans might try to help the Japanese government. The U.S. government worried that the Japanese Americans might be spies. The United States was home to Japanese Americans. They supported the United States in the war, but the U.S. government did not trust them.

Governor Carr did trust their loyalty to America. He invited Japanese Americans to come to Colorado. He offered them a place to live during the war. Other governors refused to let Japanese Americans move to their states because so many people believed that Japanese Americans were dangerous. Some said hateful things. Others said they would hurt Japanese Americans. The

Japanese Americans who lived in Colorado during World War II were not sent to live in internment camps. This group of Japanese American citizens was photographed in front of the Colorado Times *newspaper office in Denver sometime between 1916 and 1920.*

Japanese Americans in California were told to leave their homes there, but they had no place to go.

The federal government decided to force Japanese American families to live in **internment camps**. Governor Carr did not think internment camps were necessary. He thought Japanese Americans should be free citizens. All Japanese Americans who already lived in Colorado remained free citizens. Ralph Carr refused to send them to live in internment camps.

One internment camp was built in Colorado. **Amache** (ah-ma-CHAY) **Japanese Internment Camp** in Colorado was built to house Japanese Americans from California. Amache was on Colorado's eastern plains.

Courtesy DPL, Western History Collection, X-6577

Amache Japanese Internment Camp for Japanese Americans from California was built in southeastern Colorado. It quickly became Colorado's third-largest city. Japanese American families were forced to live in camps like Amache during World War II.

The area was covered with sagebrush and rattlesnakes. The government set up **army housing**. Barbed wire and armed soldiers surrounded the camp. Soon after it was built, 10,000 Japanese American men, women, and children lived at the camp.

Most people did not want any Japanese American people in Colorado. Governor Carr urged the people of Colorado to treat the Japanese people as their neighbors. He offered friendship to them. He gave a speech to a group of angry and frightened people.

Governor Carr said, "The Japanese are protected by the same constitution that protects us. An American citizen of Japanese **descent** has the same rights as any other citizen. If you harm them, you must harm me. Racial hatred threatens the happiness of you and you and you." He also said, "In Colorado, they will have full protection."

Governor Carr was firm in his belief that Japanese Americans should be treated as all other Americans. Governor Carr asked the Japanese Americans at Amache Japanese Internment Camp to help harvest Colorado's crops. Many farm-workers were fighting in the war, and farmers needed help. He made sure Japanese Americans were paid the same amount of money for their work as other farm workers. He set a good example when he hired a Japanese American to work as his housekeeper. He continued to speak against the internment camps and for Japanese American rights.

In 1942, Ralph Carr decided to run for United States senator instead of governor. It was a close race, but he lost the election. Many people thought he lost because of his support of Japanese Americans. He returned to work as a lawyer. Even though he lost the election, he stayed involved in Colorado politics.

In 1950, Ralph Carr decided to be a candidate for governor again. Only 30 days before the election, Ralph Carr died of diabetes at the age of 62. Colorado flags flew at **half-mast** the next day. Thousands of people came to the Colorado State Capitol to walk by his casket. Colorado Governor Johnson said, "Colorado has lost a great man."

Thousands of people walked by Ralph Carr's open casket in the Colorado State Capitol. He was remembered as a person who fought for justice.

Ralph Carr's Legacy

Ralph Carr's attitude toward the Japanese
Americans proved to be right. There never was
any case in which Japanese Americans spied
for Japan. Japanese American soldiers fought
bravely for the United States during World
War II.

In 1988, 44 years after World War II, the
U.S. government apologized to the Japanese
American people for forcing them to live
in internment camps. The government
apologized for the **racism** and discrimination
Japanese Americans faced during World War
II. President Ronald Reagan said, "We admit a
wrong."

In 1999, the *Denver Post* chose one person to
name Person of the Century. Out of all the
extraordinary Coloradans, the newspaper staff
chose Ralph Carr. The paper selected him

because he stood up for what was right, even when it was not popular.

Japanese Americans in Colorado remembered the man who stood up for their rights. They placed a statue of him in Sakura Square in downtown Denver. In another tribute, the city of Denver named a new courthouse in honor of Ralph Carr.

In another part of Denver, a plaque in the Colorado State Capitol says this about Ralph Carr:

Dedicated to Governor Ralph Carr a wise, humane man,
not influenced by hysteria and bigotry directed against the Japanese Americans during World War II.
By his humanitarian efforts, no Colorado resident of Japanese ancestry
was deprived of his basic freedoms, and when no others would accept the

Japanese American citizens of Colorado paid to have this statue of Ralph Carr put up in Sakura Square in downtown Denver. It honors the governor who helped them during World War II.

evacuated West Coast Japanese,
except for confinement in internment camps,
Governor Carr opened the doors and
welcomed them to Colorado.
The spirit of his deeds will live in the hearts of
true Americans.

Presented October 1974
by the Japanese Community and the Oriental
Culture Society of Colorado

Questions to Think About

- How did Ralph Carr help his poor family when he was only six?

- Which president of the United States was Ralph Carr's friend?

- What kindnesses did Ralph Carr show to Japanese Americans who were sent to Colorado during World War II?

Questions for Young Chautauquans

- Why am I (or should I be) remembered in history?

- What hardships did I face and how did I overcome them?

- What is my historical context (what else was going on in my time)?

Glossary

Amache (pronounced ah-ma-CHAY)
Japanese Internment Camp: camp built near Granada in southeastern Colorado. Japanese Americans from California were forced to live there during World War II. The camp was named for a Native American leader.

Army housing: basic living quarters or shelter provided to soldiers by the army.

Attorney general: chief law officer of a state or country.

Democracy: belief in or practice of the idea that all people are socially equal and also government by the people, especially rule of the majority.

Descent: origin of a person's parents or older members of a family.

Devotions: strong feelings of affection or dedication.

Discrimination: treating others unfairly because of their race or something else about them that they cannot change.

Ethical: following accepted rules of what is right and wrong.

Half-mast: when flags are raised only halfway up the flagpole to remember an important person who has died.

Immigrants: people who leave one country to settle in another country.

Internment camps: camps set up in the western United States to relocate Japanese American citizens from the West Coast. The ten camps had barracks for families to live in and were surrounded by armed guards.

Japanese Americans: people of Japanese ancestry who were born in the United States or have become American citizens. Japanese Americans are American citizens.

Liberty: having the freedom to do as one pleases within the law.

Loyalties: strong feelings of support for someone or for a cause, country, or organization.

Pearl Harbor: location of a naval base in Hawaii where the U.S. government stored boats, airplanes, and military equipment.

Prejudice: judgment, assumption, or opinion not based on fact. Prejudice can lead to hate, fear, or distrust of people or groups.

Racism: dislike or hatred of others based on their race.

World War II: war that lasted from 1939 to 1945. The United States fought against Japan, Germany, and Italy. The United States, along with Great Britain, France, and the Soviet Union won the war in 1945.

Timeline

1887
Ralph Carr was born in
Rosita, Colorado.

1905
Ralph graduated from
Cripple Creek High School.
Ralph entered the University
of Colorado.

1912
Ralph graduated from
the University of Colorado
Law School.

1913
Ralph married Gretchen
Fowler.

1913–1916
Ralph worked as lawyer and
newspaper writer.

1916–1924
Ralph opened a law office
in Antonito. He moved to
Denver to work as assistant
attorney general.

1927
Ralph was appointed
U.S. attorney.

1937
Gretchen Carr died
suddenly.

Timeline

1938
Ralph was elected
governor of Colorado

1940
Ralph was re-elected
governor of Colorado.

1941
Japan attacked
Pearl Harbor.

1942–1945
Japanese Americans were
forced to live in
internment camps.

1942
Ralph was defeated in
election for U.S. Senate.

1948
Ralph married
Eleanor Fairall.

1943–1949
Ralph worked in Rangely,
Colorado, as lawyer and
newspaper writer.

1950
Ralph considered running
for governor of Colorado.
Ralph died at age 62
from diabetes.

Bibliography

Amole, Gene. "Insightful Guv Gets Hero's Vote." *Rocky Mountain News*, December 10, 1987.

Briggs, Bill. "Century Standout: Gov. Ralph Carr Opposed Japanese Internment." *Denver Post*, December 27, 1999.

Carr, Ralph. "Colorado's Part in the War Effort." *The Colorado State Federation of Labor, 1942 Yearbook*. Denver Public Library Western History documents.

Carr, Ralph. "Correspondence Files." http://www.colorado.gov/dpa/doit/archives/wwcod/granada4.htm.

Castellano, John S. "Governor Ralph L. Carr: A Remembrance." *The Colorado Lawyer*, December 1991.

Harvey, Robert. *Amache: The Story of Japanese Internment in Colorado during World War II*. Dallas: Taylor Trade Publishing, 2004.

Lamm, Richard, and Duane Smith. *Pioneers and Politicians: Colorado Governors in Profile*. Golden, Colorado: Fulcrum Publishing, 2008.

Marganzino, Pasquale. "Ralph Carr Dies! His Passing Tangles State GOP Politics." *Rocky Mountain News*, September 23, 1950.

Sakurai, Gail. *Japanese American Internment Camps—Cornerstones of Freedom, Second Series*. New York: Scholastic Press, 2002.

Schrager, Adam. "He Stood Up While Others Sat." *Denver Post*, March 3, 2008.

Schrager, Adam. *The Principled Politician: The Ralph Carr Story.* Golden, Colorado: Fulcrum Publishing, 2008.

Wei, William. "Simply a Question of Patriotism: Governor Ralph L. Carr and the Japanese Americans." *Colorado Heritage Magazine*, Winter 2002.

Wood, Richard E. *Here Lies Colorado: Fascinating Figures in Colorado History*. Helena, Montana: Farcountry Press, 2005.

Index

Bibliography/Index

About This Series

In 2008, Colorado Humanities and Denver Public Schools' Social Studies Department began a partnership to bring Colorado Humanities' Young Chautauqua program to DPS and to create a series of biographies of Colorado historical figures written by teachers for young readers. The project was called "Writing Biographies for Young People." Filter Press joined the effort to publish the biographies in 2010.

Teachers attended workshops, learned from Colorado Humanities Chautauqua speakers and authors, and toured three major libraries in Denver: The Hart Library at History Colorado, the Western History/Genealogy Department in the Denver Public Library, and the Blair-Caldwell African American Research Library. Their goal was to write biographies using the same skills we ask of students: identify and locate high-quality sources for research, document those sources, and choose appropriate information from the resources.

What you hold in your hands now is the culmination of these teachers' efforts. With this set of age-appropriate biographies, students will be able to read and research on their own, learning valuable skills of research and writing at a young age. As they read each biography, students gain knowledge and appreciation of the struggles and hardships overcome by people from our past, the time period in which they lived, and why they should be remembered in history.

Knowledge is power. We hope this set of biographies will help Colorado students know the excitement of learning history through biography.

Information about the series can be obtained from any of the three partners:

Filter Press at www.FilterPressBooks.com

Colorado Humanities at www.ColoradoHumanities.org

Denver Public Schools at http://curriculum.dpsk12.org

Acknowledgments

Colorado Humanities and Denver Public Schools acknowledge the many contributors to the Great Lives in Colorado History series. Among them are the following:

The teachers who accepted the challenge of writing the biographies

Margaret Coval, Executive Director, Colorado Humanities

Josephine Jones, Director of Programs, Colorado Humanities

Betty Jo Brenner, Program Coordinator, Colorado Humanities

Michelle Delgado, K–5 Social Studies Coordinator, Denver Public Schools

Elma Ruiz, K–5 Social Studies Coordinator, Denver Public Schools, 2005–2009

Joel' Bradley, Project Coordinator, Denver Public Schools

Translation and Interpretation Services Team, Multicultural Outreach Office, Denver Public Schools

Nelson Molina, ELA Professional Development Trainer/Coach and School Liaison, Denver Public Schools

John Stansfield, storyteller, writer, and Teacher Institute lead scholar

Tom Meier, author and Arapaho historian

Celinda Reynolds Kaelin, author and Ute culture expert

National Park Service, Bent's Old Fort National Historic Site

Daniel Blegen, author and Bent's Fort expert

Blair-Caldwell African American Research Library

Coi Drummond-Gehrig, Denver Public Library, Western History/Genealogy Department

Jennifer Vega, Stephen H. Hart Library, History Colorado

Dr. Bruce Paton, author and Zebulon Pike expert

Dr. Tom Noel, author and Colorado historian

Susan Marie Frontczak, Chautauqua speaker and Young Chautauqua coach

Mary Jane Bradbury, Chautauqua speaker and Young Chautauqua coach

Dr. James Walsh, Chautauqua speaker and Young Chautauqua coach

Richard Marold, Chautauqua speaker and Young Chautauqua coach

Doris McCraw, author and Helen Hunt Jackson subject expert

Kathy Naples, Chautauqua speaker and Doc Susie subject expert

Tim Brenner, editor

Debra Faulkner, historian and archivist, Brown Palace Hotel

Kathleen Esmiol, author and Teacher Institute speaker

Vivian Sheldon Epstein, author and Teacher Institute speaker

Reconocimientos